DATE		
JUL 19 1988	SEP 1 7 1993	
FEB 26 1990	MAR 8 1994	
MAR 1 0 1990	AUG 2 3 1994	
MAR 2 1 1990		
NOV 1 0 1990	JAN 1 6 1995	
NOV 5 1991	Mar. 22 '95	
APR 1 6 1992		
MAY 1 2 1992		
AUG 6 1992		
MAY 1 0 1993		
JUL 9 1993		

TAKING CARE OF YOUR

HAMSTER

Joyce Pope

Series consultant: Michael Findlay

Photographs by: Sally Anne Thompson
and R T Willbie/Animal Photography

Franklin Watts
London   New York   Toronto   Sydney

The author

Joyce Pope is Enquiries Officer of the Zoology Department at the British Museum of Natural History and also gives regular public lectures to children and adults on a wide range of subjects.

She is involved with conservation groups and has written many books on a variety of topics including European animals, pets and town animals. She is an enthusiastic pet owner herself and currently keeps small mammals, two dogs, a cat and a horse.

The consultant

Michael Findlay is a qualified veterinary surgeon whose involvement has been mainly with pet animals. He is now an advisor to a pharmaceutical company. He is involved with Crufts Dog Show each year and is a member of the Kennel Club. He is president of several Cat Clubs and is Chairman of the Feline Advisory Bureau. He currently has three Siamese cats and two labrador dogs.

© 1986 Franklin Watts

First published in Great Britain in 1986 by Franklin Watts 12a Golden Square London W1

First published in the United States of America by Franklin Watts Inc. 387 Park Avenue South New York N.Y. 10016

UK edition: ISBN 0 86313 361 4 US edition: ISBN 0–531–10162–2 Library of Congress Catalog Card Number: 85–51602

Designed by Ben White

Illustrated by Hayward Art Group

Printed in Belgium

Acknowledgments
The photographers and publishers would like to thank Mr Neil Forbes of the Lansdown Veterinary Surgeons, Stroud; Mr Jim Rowe, Lynton Pet Shop, Gloucester and the families and their hamsters who participated in the photography for this book.

TAKING CARE OF YOUR HAMSTER

Contents

Introducing pets

People like to keep pets. They can be an interesting part of our lives. It has been proved that the company of a pet is often helpful to somebody who is alone or unwell. By caring for and watching a pet, we can find out how other creatures use the world that we think of as ours. If you remember the few important points on the next page your pet will learn to trust you and will be happy with you.

▽ Never be tempted to buy an animal that looks bedraggled, as it is difficult to cure hamster diseases. A healthy hamster will make a good pet. A sick one cannot do so.

Petkeepers' code

1 Remember that your pet is not a toy but a living creature. It has needs and feelings like hunger, contentment or fear which are similar to yours, but do not expect it to think or behave like a human.

2 Your pet depends on you for its survival, so you must care for it every day.

3 You are very much bigger than your pet, so be careful not to frighten it.

4 Your pet will need to rest at some time each day.

5 Your pet will also need to exercise and play. Make sure that it has enough room to do so.

▽ Hamsters love to explore everything around them, even your arm or the back of your neck! Although they can scamper quite fast, they do not jump and run like some other small animals, so they make very good pets for people who are disabled or who cannot move about easily.

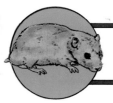

So you want a hamster?

A hamster is a good choice as a pet. It is small, so it does not take up a lot of room, yet it is not so small that it is difficult to handle. You don't have to be rich to own a hamster, as it will not cost a lot of money to buy or to keep. Hamsters are very clean, have hardly any smell and are not noisy animals, so you can keep them indoors with very little trouble.

▽ If you have other pets, you must be sure that your hamster will not be frightened by them. Most cats would look on a hamster as something to kill.

Although hamsters are easy to keep, there are several things that you must do before you get one. The most important is to make sure that everyone in your household agrees to your having one. Together you should decide where you will keep it. You must be sure that you have the time to look after it which means playing with it, feeding it and cleaning the cage each day.

You will need to get a cage and this will probably cost you some money. So will the food and bedding that the animal must have. If it becomes ill, you will have to take it to the vet and the medicines which it may need could be expensive.

▽ A hamster must be kept warm especially in the winter. Always keep it out of drafts.

△ Hamsters spend a great deal of time grooming themselves, combing their whiskers and washing their faces with their paws.

What is a hamster?

All hamsters are members of a group of furry, warm-blooded creatures called rodents. The main thing that makes rodents different from other animals is the shape of their front, or incisor, teeth, which are suitable for nibbling tough plant food. They protect themselves in the wild by living in burrows and only coming out to feed at night. They have good senses of hearing and smell. Their long whiskers help them to feel things.

△ Hamsters' teeth grow continually and hamsters will gnaw hard objects to keep them short.

▽ Hamsters use their front paws like hands to hold their food.

There are many sorts of hamsters in the world. Some, like the common European hamster, are quite big creatures, which would not be suitable to keep as pets. Others, like the dwarf Chinese hamster are sometimes seen in pet shops. But the golden hamster, which can be many colors, is the most common hamster and is by far the best type for a family pet.

▽ A hamster normally looks like a fairly dumpy creature. But if it is curious about something which it wishes to investigate without getting too close, it can stretch out to a length of about 6in (15cm).

All pet golden hamsters are said to have descended from a single female and her family which were discovered in Syria in 1930. Although we keep them in cages we must remember that golden hamsters were originally desert creatures. This helps us to understand their habits.

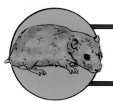
Once you have decided to keep a hamster, you must prepare a cage for it which must be made of metal or strong plastic, as a hamster will eat its way out of anything else.

You must also find a suitable part of your house in which to keep your pet. It should be fairly warm right through the year and it must be draft free. But don't put it in a place which gets direct sunlight or it will overheat.

▽ If you intend to buy or make a cage, the minimum size of the base should be 16½ × 10½in (42 × 27cm). If possible, it should have an overall height of 14in (36cm) which will give room for an upper floor to be fitted in.

You can buy many types of cages, but be sure that whatever you get gives your hamster enough space to exercise itself. The cage should contain an exercise wheel for it to play on.

You should get suitable pots and water containers for food and drink for your pet. You will also need to get some food, bedding and floor covering to furnish the cage before you put a hamster into it.

△ Circular plastic cages are draft free, but could overheat in direct sunlight. They are designed so that extra floors and 'rooms' can be added.

△ Circular cages are now very popular. They do not take up much room, and since they usually have several floors, they give the hamster space to explore.

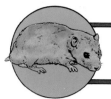

One problem that does not arise when getting a hamster is whether to get one or a pair. In the wild, hamsters always live alone. If you put more than one in a cage, they will almost always fight. It does not matter whether you get a male or a female, for either makes an equally good pet. You will find that almost all pet shops keep hamsters. Make sure that an adult goes with you, as many pet shops will not sell live animals to children.

△ In a pet shop you will be able to see plenty of hamsters so you can choose the one that you like best. Take one that looks fairly active, not one that is cowering in a corner of its cage.

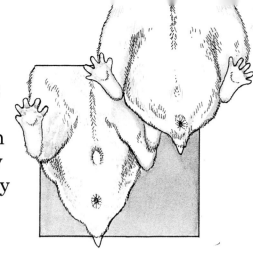

Try to buy a hamster which is about five weeks old. If you get an older one it may be difficult to tame. When you first see them, the hamsters may look a bit sleepy. Don't be worried by this, for they normally sleep during the daytime and are most active in the evening and at night.

Look for one with a glossy, well-groomed coat which has no bald patches or sores on it. Make sure that its feet are undamaged and that its nose is clean and not runny. Check that its eyes are bright and clear with no discharge and that its front teeth are growing parallel to each other. Look for the droppings in the cage. They should be dark and firm – a sign of a healthy hamster.

△ It is not very difficult to tell the sex of a hamster, even when it is young. If you look at the underside of the animal, the rear end of a female is a rounded shape and the genital opening is close to the anus. In a male, the shape is more angled and the genital opening is much further from the anus than in females.

▽ A cinnamon colored hamster.

Wild golden hamsters have yellowish-brown colored fur. Like all normal wild animals they have dark colored eyes. Since hamsters have been kept and bred in captivity, many other fur colors have occurred. Sometimes white or pale colored hamsters have pink or red eyes.

New varieties are being bred which produce different color variations of silvery-gray fur. Banded hamsters have circles of white fur breaking the base color of their bodies.

△ A piebald hamster has dark eyes and patches of different colors on a white background.

Most hamsters have fairly short-haired coats like their wild ancestors. The one above is a golden banded satin hamster. The length of the hairs which go to make up the coat is the same as normal, but each hair has a gloss which makes the coat look much finer and the colors much brighter.

A rarer type is the long haired hamster, like the black-eyed white shown on the right. This one is a satinized variety and you can see the sheen on its long hairs.

Rex hamsters are unusual. They may be any color, and they have dense, long, curly coats. Even their whiskers are curled. Baby Rex hamsters have long, wavy hair from an early age.

△ A golden banded satin hamster.

△ You should not get a long-coated hamster unless you are sure that you have plenty of time to look after it. Normal hamsters can groom themselves, but a long coat will need to be brushed daily (a soft toothbrush will do the job very well).

A new hamster at home

Before you get your hamster you should make sure whether or not the pet shop will give you a carrying case for it. If not, you should take a suitable box with you. You certainly won't be able to take a lively hamster home in your pocket!

▽ You can easily make a carrying box for a hamster or other small pet from an old cookie tin or similar sort of box, which the animal cannot gnaw through. Make air holes in the lid, starting from the inside. Then flatten the jagged edges with a hammer.

Put plenty of soft hay in it and some food, such as sunflower seeds or nuts. Carry the box home as quickly as you can, but without too much jolting. As soon as you get home, coax the hamster from its box into the cage that you have prepared for it. Try not to pick it up although you may have to if the hamster doesn't seem to want to move.

◁ Hamsters normally sleep through the day and become more active at night. Do not worry if your new pet seems to spend a great deal of its life asleep. As it gets to know you better it will probably start to wake up earlier in the day.

△ You should prepare a cage for your hamster with a sleeping area, bedding, food, water and some floor covering. A wheel for exercise is also very important.

As soon as it is in its new home, your hamster will probably look for some sort of shelter. The cage should contain a sleeping box with suitable bedding such as hay or ground corn cobs in it. You could use a flower pot on its side as a bedroom for the hamster.

Do not try to play with the animal right away. Remember that coming to live with you is a great change in its way of life and you should let it adjust slowly. Later, probably in the evening, the hamster will wake up and begin to explore.

At first it may rush back to its sleeping place if you make a noise or sudden movement near the cage. Soon it will be running round quite confidently. You can then begin to make friends with it.

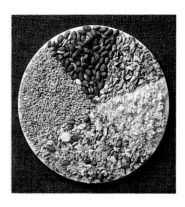

△ A hamster food mix, separated to show the flaked maize, sunflower seeds, peanuts and grain that it is made of.

A hamster needs to eat about $\frac{1}{2}$oz (15g) of food each day. This should be made up partly of dry grain and pellets and partly of fresh greens or fruit. You can buy packs of premixed hamster food from a pet shop but don't get too much at one time, or it will go stale.

It is best to feed a hamster is in the evening, when it is beginning to be active. The hamster may empty its food bowl very quickly, but is unlikely to eat it all at once. It will hide the food around the cage.

△ You should put your dry hamster food into a bowl which is quite solid or broad based so that the animal cannot tip it over or pull about the cage.

▷ A drip water container attached to the side of a cage. These containers ensure that the water does not become dirty from droppings or food getting into it.

The hamster carries things in two large pouches inside the cheeks on either side of its face. Because of its habit of hoarding, you must be careful not to give your hamster anything which will go bad quickly, or you may find that the animal has developed an upset stomach from eating decaying food.

Hamsters like to have fresh water to drink. The best sort of container is a drip bottle, which can be attached to the side of the cage. The hamster will quickly learn how to sip from it.

△ A hamster with its cheek pouches full looks swollen about the neck. It empties the food into its mouth by pushing the back of the pouches from the outside with its front paws.

As well as dry grains and nuts, you should give your hamster a wide variety of fresh plant food. This can include part of the food you buy for yourself. An outer leaf from a cabbage or lettuce or a slice from the top of a carrot will be taken quickly. So will a slice of apple or a few grapes or raisins. In fact, almost any fruit or vegetable that you think is nice is suitable for your hamster.

Do not feed it raw potatoes or citrus fruit. Don't make the helping too large, for the hamster will not be able to eat it all. Some food, especially fruit, goes moldy very quickly.

▷ Your dry hamster food should not contain too much sunflower seed, which would make the diet too rich in oil. But sunflower seeds make good tidbits, especially when you want to encourage the animal to come to you.

▽ Cultivated plants that hamsters enjoy include lettuce, spinach, cabbage, carrots, beets and apple.

Almost wherever you live, you should be able to find wild plants such as grass, dandelion and clover. Chickweed and young shoots of blackberry are good hamster food too.

Be very careful that you are not taking wild food from places that have been sprayed with insecticides, or from near a main road, where there may be a great deal of lead in the plants. You should always wash all sorts of plant food and dry it carefully, before giving it to your pet. Be very careful to identify all wild plants correctly, as some are poisonous.

▽ Wild plants include all sorts of grasses, dandelion, clover and blackberry shoots and common vetch.

Try to be patient when you first get home and let your hamster settle down in its new surroundings before you begin to handle it. The hamster might not realize that you want to be friendly and if it is frightened it may bite you.

▽ The correct way to pick up a hamster. Now you can carry the animal safely. The hamster will not try to run away because it feels secure since one of your hands is below it and the other makes a sort of tunnel over it.

It may take several days before your pet is sure that you do not mean it any harm. Hold out a sunflower seed or piece of cheese and sooner or later the hamster will approach to take it from your fingers. When it looks for a treat as soon as it sees you, you know that it will be confident enough to be picked up.

▷ When you play with a hamster it can move quite quickly. You must be very careful not to frighten it by grabbing at it. If you do so it might bite you.

In a short time your hamster will know you well. Let it approach and smell your fingers. Stroke it softly and then gently scoop it up in both hands. Let it sit there but do not squeeze it. Allow it to run back into its cage when it wishes.

Later, when it is used to being held you can pick it up with one hand around its body and support it with the other hand. Be very careful if you carry it about and do not hold it too tightly as you could hurt it badly. Never, never drop a hamster. They are easily injured by a fall.

△ Try to discover which are your hamster's favorite foods. Offer it bits of all sorts of food, except for chocolate, which can clog its pouches.

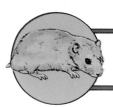

Play and exercise

Although your hamster may have a large enough cage and plenty to eat, it will like to explore and investigate things. You can add to the variety of its life by playing with it.

Once you can pick it up and handle it safely, you can let it out of its cage. It is wise to make an enclosure so that it does not hide behind furniture or under the floorboards where you could not get it back.

▽ A run like this is easy to make. You can put different things, such as some big twigs of wood in there for it to explore. Finding out how your hamster reacts to new things will help you to understand its world better.

Hamsters cannot jump well, so you can make a temporary run with quite low walls which should prevent an escape. Make sure that there are no cats or dogs about, as they would frighten and possibly kill your hamster.

Another way to let your pet explore is to give it an exercise ball. This may be on a stand or it can be put on the floor and the hamster will be able to travel about but can't escape. At first, put the hamster in the exercise ball for a few minutes. Later you can leave it in there for up to one hour.

△ Your hamster needs plenty of exercise even in its cage. The best way to see that it gets this it to give it a wheel. This should have a solid rim and back, or your pet may hurt itself.

Cover the floor of your hamster's cage with some sheets of newspaper. Add a layer of peat, then wood shavings and then sawdust about 1in (2.5cm) deep. If your hamster digs down and tears up the paper, remove it, as newsprint can be poisonous.

The sleeping place should have hay or shredded paper. Hamsters tend to eat their bedding and some man-made fibers are very bad for them. Ask for advice at the pet shop.

△ You can encourage your hamster to use a particular place as a lavatory by putting a little soiled floor covering into a shallow dish when you clean the cage out. The hamster will get used to using this area.

It is easy to empty droppings from a small container, such as the lid of a jar, when you clean the cage.

Hamsters, like all animals that live in burrows, are very clean animals, using one small corner of their living space as a lavatory. This means that it can be cleaned out easily each day. About every two weeks all of the bedding and floor covering should be taken out and replaced with fresh bedding.

Once a month the cage should be scrubbed out but allow it to dry out thoroughly before returning the hamster. Feeding bowls and the water container should be thoroughly washed each week.

△ A hamster will wash itself repeatedly while sitting on its hindquarters. They are very clean animals and seem to enjoy their thorough grooming process.

◁ You need to remove the hamster when you "spring clean" its cage. This is a good time to put it into its exercise ball but remember that even its toys will need cleaning from time to time.

Hamsters seldom survive for more than two or three years. You can help to keep your pet free from illness by providing proper housing and diet. A hamster needs space to exercise and plenty of vitamins in its food.

Hamsters can catch infections from human beings, so if you are ill you should get somebody else to feed and clean out your pet's cage.

△ A hamster may run into danger if it escapes from its cage, so you should catch it as quickly as possible. A jar trap like the one above is an easy way of trapping a hamster that does not want to be caught. You should creep up to the jar trap very quietly and gently cup your hand over the open end.

If your hamster seems to be unwell, you should take it to the vet. As you clean the cage out you should look for signs of constipation or diarrhea. Constipation may be cured in young hamsters by making sure that they have plenty of water and moistened green vegetables. Diarrhea may be a symptom of several other diseases.

Alway wash your hands when you have been playing with your hamster or cleaning out the cage. There is then less chance of passing any infection from your pet to the family.

▽ A visit to the vet can often save a pet's life. Illness in small animals often develops very fast, so don't wait to see if it gets better on its own – it probably won't!

Two common reasons for visiting the vet are overgrown claws, which need clipping, or overgrown teeth, which are the result of a hamster not having enough hard things to gnaw with its incisor teeth.

Checklist

 Daily

1 Check water level in container. Refill if necessary.
2 Feed hamster, in evening only.
3 Remove droppings from lavatory area.
4 Remove any obviously soiled bedding.
5 Check bedding level and add more if needed.
6 Check health of the hamster – fur shining, eyes bright etc. Groom if necessary.
7 Wash food bowls and water bottle carefully. Do this separately and use different cloths from those used for the family washing up.

 Weekly

1 Clean out all beddingand put in replacement bedding.
2 Wash out water bottle or bowl.
3 Check that you have enough food to last you for the coming week. Buy more if necessary.

 Occasionally

1 Empty cage completely and scrub it out using hot water with a little disinfectant in it. Make sure you rinse it thoroughly and dry it well.
2 Wash all toys etc and make sure that you rinse them well. Any smell may put your pet off using them again.
3 Check claw and tooth growth. Take the animal to the vet if necessary, to have these attended to.
4 Remember to get seeds to sow in your garden or window box to give your pet fresh food.

A hamster diary

It is often difficult to recall exactly how your hamster looked when you first got it. For example, how quickly it grew or how long it took to become tame. The best way to remember these things is to keep a hamster diary.

All you need is a book in which you can write down everything that you notice about your pet. Weigh it in the carrying box when you first get it. Then weigh the box empty. The difference equals the weight of your pet. You can check its growth as it gets older and when it is tame you will be able to weigh it without the box.

Watch your pet and note all the things that it does everyday. Write the date at the top of all your observations. Then you will be able to see if your hamster's behavior changes as it grows older.

Your hamster diary could make a very good school project. By observing your pet regularly you will learn more about it and be able to care better for it.

Index

PRINTED IN BELGIUM BY

proost
INTERNATIONAL BOOK PRODUCTION